This Momentary World

Poems by Jody Stewart

NINE MILE BOOKS

Publisher: Nine Mile Art Corp.
Editors: Bob Herz, Stephen Kuusisto, Andrea Scarpino
Cover Art: Taylor Home, in Conway, Massachusetts, 1955.
Author photo: E.J.Cothey
Cover photo: Charles H. Taylor, jr.

Nine Mile Books is an imprint of Nine Mile Art Corp.
The publishers gratefully acknowledge support of the New York State
Council on the Arts with the support of Governor Andrew M. Cuomo and
the New York State Legislature. We also acknowledge support of the
County of Onondaga and CNY Arts through the Tier Three Project Support
Grant Program. We have also received significant support from the Central
New York Community Foundation. This publication would not have been
possible without the generous support of these groups. We are very grateful
to them all.

ISBN: 979-8-9871927-2-6

ACKNOWLEDGMENTS

I am grateful to the small presses and their editors in which a number of these poems first appeared, many in different, and rougher versions. My thanks to: Stratis Haviaris of Arion's Dolphin; Bob MacNamara, L'Epervier Press; Rolly Kent, Maguey Press; David Spicer, raccoon/Ion Books; Ron Slate, Chowder Chapbooks; the collected editors of Alice James Books; Bin Ramke for selecting "The Red Window" for University of George Press; Jack Estes, Pleasure Boat Studio; Anthony Howell and Kerry Lee Powell, Grey Suit Editions; *Ploughshares*, V. 6, # 4, 1981 for "October"; and thank you everyone at Nine Mile for giving these poems a new body.

My gratitude as well to The John Simon Guggenheim Memorial Foundation, the Hawthornden fellowships, Massachusetts Cultural Council and the Elizabeth George Foundation for their recognition and support. Thanks also to countless people! (I would mess if up if I attempted to recall and thank everyone; there have been so many kindnesses over the last 4 & decades.) I am grateful to Jan Freeman for not only her own poetry, but her professional expertise and support in helping shape this selection, to Juliet Schulman-Hall for the typing and fashioning of the pages and for a new friendship which I value so much! And to Susan Aizenberg, a a terrific poet and friend, and the best Nagger-in-Chief! To my sister/housemate, Jill. Gratitude particularly to my first "teachers" Ellen Voight and Norman Dubie; due to their wisdom and kindnesses I was able to understand how much I wanted/needed to learn more about writing, reading and just doing the work! It made all the difference.

I am compelled to mention a few more writers, muses and friends whose advice, friendship and support have contributed both to daily living and getting down to work from the '70's to pulling this book together in the last few years. In no particular order my gratitude to: Cynthia Hogue, Alane Rollings, Anthony Howell, MK, Mary Bruce, Tim Liu, the No Name Writers (currently Bob, Doug, Jim, and Kirsten,) Hannah Dubie, Carolyn Cushing, Mark Rovere and other Barlovians, Anene Tressler-Hauschultz, Bob Herz, Natalie Walker, my wonderful late aunt (for whom I was named) Pamela Taylor Wetzels, Paul Sharits, Margaret Lloyd, John Barnie, the Conway House, Sharon Mayberry, Adam Walton, Brenda Peterson, Jim

Cervantes, Leigh Franks and so many more people, places, dogs, my years in St. Ives and the whole Farm where I am blessed to live.
(in the poem Pocumtuck Watch, the phrase " Heathens and Savages" is a direct quote from the Reverend Williams' diary. As a man of his time, church, and settlement that's what he wrote.)

for Rarie Taylor Dye, 1925-2016 —Mom
you were so much more than I realized!

and with most affectionate memory, dear poet-friends:
Lee Holleman McCarthy, Colette Inez, David Spicer

Contents

Foreword

Why a Selected and not a New and Selected? There were raised eyebrows! Well, reviewing work and self, I realized I didn't want a N&S. For me there's a wholeness to this array of earlier work, its progress, its failures, its romanticism, youth, losses, good times, and failures. It's my own flawed concerto.

I'm older now. Yay! I love being older; a bee in the center of a zinnia is a fine event. I am fortunate. I've worn a cloak of "white privilege" always, with a vague recognition but no particular language for it. I was just getting by like everyone else, but many *everyone elses* have had it a lot harder than me. One learns some of that as a life progresses, but I'll never get all of it. Like many girls, I lived without a father; when and where I grew up a working single mother was the social exception. My father, who became a wonderful Dad to others, was imaginary to me. I felt out of balance (what kid doesn't?)—fancy blue- blood stuff via my Grandmother's family, a mysterious Mormon heritage via the paternal side. Perhaps this was the source of my "romantic" irresponsibility, a choice of course out of which I committed many unkindnesses—but it sure informed my earlier work! I was born able bodied and more of less continue to be so. That also was the luck of the draw. There is so much I'd like to understand better, but I didn't realize how much *much* is out there!

Onward!

—Pamela (Jody) Stewart, 2022

Tansy, Wormwood, Sage

Who watered these greens
and greys? Who cut
and dried to feed her sheep in winter?
Who touched the red bull's neck?
It doesn't matter, but I felt her
as the herbs were cut today.
The faded clapboard house
warmed with October's sun.
It doesn't matter, but I stood there
one moment more exact than ever
returning home.

from *The Figure Eight at Midnight,*
The Hawley Road Marsh Marigolds,
The St. Vlas Elegies, 1975-1977

THE HAWLEY ROAD MARSH MARIGOLDS

for Hannah

April returns this constellation of flowers
in a ditch, butter-shadows with green orbs
on water. Sometimes we eat them, our details
of morning. Little lights strung
in a black mirror inside us. The mirror is
inside us, not, as we thought, in the faces
of our children looking back, and up, even into

our eyes. The ditch widens in winter.
I once painted a small boy skating on it
out of these glazed willows in a blue coat.
He had yellow gloves and was visible just
for a moment this side of the trees. I've lost
the idea of him. His bright hand in black water is
the curve of my own wet arm.
There is a little girl who lives with me, not

inside me, but here with us. Everything
scares me. Once she was just yours,
your idea of someone skating a distance
when there were no details. Now,
everything is ours and these incidents of love
scare me. They are specific like that unexpected swarm
of yellow stars.

DISMISSALS

If these walks by the lake will calm us
like these lovers we dismiss as children
& good soldiers.
—David St. John

I

Outside is the call of red
hollyhocks bending
in shade against the wall.
When an eye closes, the ear
begins to hear the sound of her long
hair falling. She
has been leaning at the window and
has just climbed out. Someone
unlocking the room brings water
and a comb for the lame girl, no
longer there, who's crouching
in the garden and, with rough fingers,
digs a hole in which to plant
her longest leg, her head
bent, red hair falling to her knees.

II

Those fingerprints on glass she's
left, going out of the house. A young
girl becoming brave walks down
Chestnut Street to the mews with a small
sack of flour under her coat.
She will powder those few, timid faces
brought up from Charleston, and
learn to set a yellow bonnet
on the woman's head. She spreads
a brown cloak across their knees; soon,

in a carriage, they are moving North out
of Philadelphia. Later her supper is soup,
bread and chocolate. Before bed
she returns barefoot with a soft rag
and wipes clean the smudged
glass, black now and very cold.

III

for Mary Lou Wittig

Now the one I'm thinking of comes with
adagio in a case.
Unfolding her music stand at twilight,
she twists the bell
into place. It is correct,
when stars appear, to warm up:
her own mouth, the horn, to ask the moon
to make things ready by holding still.
No one is dreaming of this woman
because the dream's outside
keeping time. The first movement's
almost a cadence, but is taken up
by open windows. The apple trees
have stopped their prettiness and shifted
into leaves.

IV

Sometime in Greece, the soldiers
slowly walking up the path through
a grove of dusty olive trees,
come to the shrine they've
been searching for. Across the valley
are the sounds of war cracking;
someone dropping a hammer
on stones. A saint stands alone
in the clearing, his blue face lifted.

While his finger points
at the clouded sky, a stone lantern rests
against his knees. Each man stopping
briefly, moves his hand from forehead
to chest, and nods. Eyes closed a moment
before continuing. Then a sudden
louder noise and the saint rises
up where he'd been looking; the lantern
falls to pieces on the ground.
When the dust settles, soldiers filing past
continue with their silent prayers, and remember

the sound of a painted hand, real and falling
through the leaves.

DESERT PLANTS FOR EDITH WHARTON'S FORGOTTEN WOMEN: 1876

Your last dowager stands in a room
with circlets of white flowers that are,
like her tiny hands,
emerging from their sleeves. You think
such generosity in a monster, and look beyond

to where the young ocotillos flaunt their triumphs
brief as those of the women you've invented. Their waxy,
scarlet cones are balanced
like torches against a night sky.

The women who travel stop a moment
where lavender verbenas glow that color of iris
in a Massachusetts dusk. They stoop
and brush a purple cloud away to find,
face down, a gilt-edged mirror
which lost its place to necessities:
a water barrel or sack
of mesquite beans. This mirror was discarded

that once loved the world of gardenias
in a bride's hair and the first attack
at the footstep of that lover who's just become a husband.
You remember your brief genius
for feeling how these women
gathered in crowded rooms. They are, now,
night-blooming flowers relaxing

like heavy fruit to a use
at the end of moisture; these flowers
decorate a mirror which is haunted
by women who are aging, who
might now be wading in a river or touching

a spray of apple blossoms to an arm and breast. Or

they could be one woman
you never imagined, tired and
stepping from a wagon into a desert looking to the horizon,
making a study of it.

POCUMTUCK WATCH

I

Frontispiece

The last lining has been scrubbed
from her eye. She sees
that her father no longer rides
that old horse drinking at the river,
but is the horse.
The same river where one summer
a man put a knife
into the chest of his daughter,
very hard and sure of himself.

Now, where rocks show,
the horse straddles the river.
Late August and few fish
are left. The horse,
and what he was, could be a bridge
saving her feet from those sharp
edges. But like the old story
the horse walks across himself
and trots away.

II
The Book: February 29, 1704

The snow's crust brings them right up
over the wall. Winter dawn,
there isn't to be any sun at all
that day, and the children
not allowed to play are dropped,
with little air, into sacks of flour.
A few, remaindered from the smoke,
live to settle with aunts
or older brothers.

In the cellar, women passing musket balls
aren't fast enough; the men
so busy firing they don't hear
any of them enter from the back.
Two infants thrown on floor stones, the barns
in flame, snow melting off the roofs
and the singed horses
explode against their stalls
until there are no stalls.

The Reverend Williams dragged
from his bed yells 'Heathens and Papists!'
A knife at his back, they push
him down the stairs. Two
of his children dead in the hall.
But weak-kneed Eunice coming
from the kitchen, dries
the morning milk from her hands
and hooking her mind's eye
to Providence, never makes a noise.

Northward. So cold and long
a walk. The ailing easily split.
Heathens, not the French, carry
the little children and give

20

their captives tight-stitched shoes.
The Reverend Williams holds
his Bible like a heart, and with good
grace his wife sends him
on ahead. Wading the Green River
she trips, her forehead kissing
a rock and from behind
the axe is quick. Blood on ice
reminds him of summer desserts.
A *savage* ties him in snowshoes
and all the way are prayers
and something that soonest grows old
which he calls Thanks.

His eldest daughter was most
entirely lost. They smooth her
in bear grease, her lips
shining with a strange taste;
they put her in skins and furs
and take the mother's name away.
Her prayers are Latin, shells
in her ears. At night she fingers both
sets of beads. Later, when she could,
she didn't come back, not even
when her father asked.

III
The Letter

"Still, this isn't the worst
sort of story. Just as the white
gases of dead plantations linger
in unlikely places, there's cruelty
outside our vigils. Some losses are
equivalent. There's always one thing left
that might be shared."

She turns her eye from stories back
to the river. The dusk already has made
the water black, and the rocks lose
their luster. No longer knives
but rounded clubs dropped behind,
or the open heads of mothers.
Across the river, a dim farmhouse
blinks on and two horses stand
by the pasture gate. Identical shapes
that face each other. She's heard before
that two horses ate each other
in the night. She will watch
for this, preventing nothing,
watch because the water's moving,
the blood done feeding the largest fish,
already caught and eaten years ago.

HAPLOSCOPE

There is a red, invisible flower
that is dishonest and sometimes shows
from another side
as purple in the autumn bogs at night.
It's a dreadful, violent marsh-lamp
glowing behind the eyes of a woman
who's suddenly shocked

and emptied of herself. She is simple
to look at; bare arms and knees, everything
expected, even the black
and violet shadows in her eyes. She isn't
you or me or the bouquet
of roses in her mother's hall, but

like the single burnt cloud at evening
that spills red and golden snow across the fields,
she sings to her husband and daughter of a sunset
with white stars, of the red
physical trees growing up beside her.

THE FIGURE EIGHT AT MIDNIGHT

A husband is out on the savannas hunting
birds while his dog
streaks through the grass and three
small boys watch from a hillside. Who
would want him back, the hunter
or what he kills? His young wife
lights a fire, waiting supper for her sons.
She pours custard
into blue bowls, her arrangement
of a little hope. No one has asked

for this story. Somewhere
she becomes another woman expecting nothing.
A man, who has shaved for the first
time in years, sees her through a window
winding a large brass clock. Maybe
he'll rap his cane on the glass
and begin speaking, or
perhaps just continue past her,
down to a field to sit
in the shade of a pear tree. The one

he ate from as a boy. He could be a doctor,
or a painter discerning that
all our world is color and cruelty, a skin,
under the skin that is gorgeous and elemental.
By selecting flowers for each room

she admits all the hard work
of a calendar; doesn't it suggest
the bright pictures of a book found
in a child's cupboard, one at a time
fading? To be replaced
with what? With expecting nothing and
the choice to continue as, outside
the window, there remains the face

of a man, and a few words. The woman puts back
the key to her clock. It might be
early morning and the shy birds slipping
from the trees into the sunlight, sing
for someone in the yard who's
rubbing the dust from a pear, who is familiar.

BERLIN WINTER 1931

She was all white and red in the lights
of morning, running to the one-eyed man
and his cart of snails.
A circular cut, flesh falling
from the shell, she'd dip her fingers
in the broth and bite,
then bite again. It was all she'd eat
then the whole day she'd be sleeping. I'd hear
her cough in the blue city air.
The streets were full
of the white blouses of wives, their skirts
working through the stalls, pale vegetables
and fish for their baskets. Our days
were all sleep and exchange. At night

we were splinters and fountains; we were red
and black and lavender. Nothing
that was beautiful was cold. We had no
landscapes. We loved our poppies at dusk
and ate fruit with salt. Sometimes,
at dawn, I walked in the park collecting
fresh linden flowers off the trees.
They'd dry by the fire
and we'd drink for supper. The night she died
I woke to the smell of milk spilled
on the gas ring. The best spoon still hot.
her throat was blue, her eyes two soft knots
pulled up above her mouth which was still
red and white. All those flowers sent
by men. I spent the whole day in the smell
of lime. I saw her first
that day in the shop, opened the door
where she was dressing. Once I had seen her
dance with just a black feather. She was water
and heat, a white arch in the night
that invented all of us.

There is a scarred piano in a warehouse
which reminds me of those days. Now, in summer,
it's rolled out on the broken streets and someone
plays the old songs wasted
on those new young girls, on infants
and husbands. There are no more nights
displacing our days. Here a sip of tea, there
a red flower at a window and some bricks.
Just moments. The copper fish
still hang in the markets. A lovely wife
fingers a carp and brushes the hair
back from her neck. I imagine her
an oval nude in her kitchen heating
water at midnight and humming a tune
she passed like a stranger in the street.

ESTATES

I am noticing from my window how the grass
must be startled by my sister lifting
bundles of straw to spread over
the carrots and turnips. November,
and last evening it was Father
who saw it first, down on the common. He
ran across to sound the church bells.
Everyone coming out of their houses
from supper onto the lawns
watched the sky. Purple
and bronze, unlike any jewels or cloth I know.
I saw it from this window, the way the trees
were black and terrible within this radiance.

It's some time now that a man moved out
beyond any approaches. Distance is most severe
yet he does exist unlike the blue, frozen faces
brought up from the South. Those losses
can be named and placed, perhaps
beside a little sister wrapped in white satin.

And what is my service? I am not
what they think. God, keep us from what they call households!
We are the brittle sisters. A carriage at the door
and whoever knocks belongs to someone
who's supposed to be me—but if they think
of me at all, it isn't me.

DAGUERREOTYPE

This is not a dream that she might have:
a picture of his family on a picnic
by the waterfall in summer.
The children's hats are placed
on the rocks away from the pool
and everyone is laughing but cannot hear
themselves above the noise of the falls.
The youngest has dropped his cake
in the water. A white cake with raisins.
He walks away

from the river grabbing at the curled
bark of trees, throwing stones.
Later that evening a fishing boat slips
back up the river, is beached and the man
out of his boat is tired and must care for himself.

At the church the candles have been replaced;
a woman runs a cloth along the rails,
humming to herself and thinking tomorrow
she must cut yellow flowers for her table. Today
she is watching her daughter bathe
at a basin, breasts collecting in a shadow
as the girl bends, water faintly blue
against white enamel. Her child, suddenly poured
and unfamiliar. Across sunlight
the shadow of a bird stains the wood.
Everything is still and very clean.

Tomorrow is the daughter's birthday and at dawn
begins the tradition of the necklace.
Her father must spend the day away
from water, in the fields gathering daisies,
yarrow and angel pine from the forest's edge.
He'll sit on a stone in the orchard

and chew wintergreen, tying that necklace,
sprinkling it with water from the blue bottle at his waist.

None of this belongs to the woman
walking back alone through the fields to a house
where no one is waiting. Once there was a man
who cut pine boughs in winter to cover
her roses, then banked the house with leaves
and tar paper. Sometimes she stands
in her bath and stretches to touch
the ceiling, or the window, tracing
her name in the steam or drawing an arrow or bird
and sings to herself that someone is watching.

THE COLUMBINE FIELDS AT EASTER

Thomas James 1946-1973

It burns, this idea of red and white, a finger
pricked in snow behind a shed – a ceremony
which wishes to marry an absence
a sister, itself, or the small season
that flickers in April when the tiny
points of a wildflower we shouldn't touch
are irresistible as those old, bonewhite
fingers stitching up
the ragged breast of an ornamental dove.

It fell too many times
from the Easter branch by the door
surviving, after all, its first self
as sawdust and crushed glass. The pale columbine

by the edge of the woods dips its beak
like a needle in the mouth of a dead bird
that drills
through the diamond wreckage of someone
whose hollow bones spilled out all the words
of a visit, or flight across a dappled field
with water and ice that's torn from us.
The audience

of the dead is our most demanding, a soft
flower bell that can't endure us, or
this fire from nowhere:
a flock of returning birds
that drops down on our meadow to be fed

by God, by men weaving through the gate
from the woods as though a thin seam
bound our worlds of light and dark, that are
these bundles of flaming columbine, gentle
in our arms like the bodies of the dead.

from *THE ST. VLAS ELEGIES*

The Dead Prince

A fresh, green branch of lilac grows heavy
in the curve of its existence. Moving into
this room through candlelight, it brushes his hand
like the sleeve of the woman who is bathing
his face and neck. She has opened
the window and the whole tree

enters with its scent and moisture. He remembers
the ribbons trailing from her dress
suivez-moi jeune homme, lavender and white
he caught them while dancing and traced the first form
of his love for her. A hollow vase

is filling with flowers. Like the ribbons bunched
in his hands, there is too much of everything
outside him. Any word spoken from the next room
no longer distracts him from the curve of her arm
on the windowsill. Everything he feels

empties into the branches of a lilac tree. She
can't see what stirs in the dark leaves above her
or feel the print of their shadow
on her arm but, like us,
joins the weight of falling flowers and, like them,
she alters herself to remain
in the shade of a large lilac that stands
outside the window of a house which is filling
with a solid, undreamed of light.

Sonya

You remember that perfect night
when a mouse
jumped out of your shoe and spun around
on the flowered carpet, just for a moment,
then vanished. That moment
your whole life became invasion
and it was you
lost in the trees and singing, suddenly clear
to everyone among the flowered branches.

That Christmas night you dressed
and darkened yourself. Who
is that Circassian boy they asked,
there on the stairs,
he is so pretty! Later in the sleigh
your cousin kissed you. As someone unfamiliar
you'd never been so much yourself
to him. You should have entered the last lamp

burning in the hallway, remote
with a tender, narrow light and not climbed
the stairs dreaming
of a blue silk dress with its ordered
chain of keys. Other nights are less, are
an afternoon like this standing here in winter waiting
for lilacs to swoop down on the gate,
to bring you back into the trees, mysterious
and lucid. There wasn't affection

anywhere, but such relief
that you never really asked, that
you wrote first to him: *I have something else in mind.*

Each morning at the table
you are kissed by everyone.
They save the place for you to sit,

familiar, in your wooden chair. You pour
all the steaming water out and know
your chair was once a tree,
that once you were a boy
warmed by a boy on a snowy night.
You said *he recognized himself in me!*

The Woods

The pictures are down, the mirror
and tapestries, I've blocked
the window while outside snow falls
like hundreds of white flowers
within an orchard at midnight. The people

down the road have pulled the rags
from harness-bells. They drive
away, a soft figure threading shut
cold petals behind them. Once
I told you that music was visual
and solid, that it arranged the objects
in a room. I wasn't wrong.
Tonight I refuse a mirror
while dressing. It's Christmas.
The white candle is steady beside
the glass bowl, clean and filled

with cool water. The water
is heavy and still. I dress
as though I were another woman
who has never entered this room. My hair piled
to a lantern which will trace any
dark eye running to nose
and mouth. You bring
hot wax and a spoon. The wax drops

through water with a slow,
stiff movement throwing new shadows
on the wall. Do you see them describe us?
This is still our room, ordinary
and objective, but the shapes that reflect
us are unfamiliar. If tonight I enter
the words of your new dream I am the first
sound from a strange face, just Natasha
turning towards you in memory, the return

of small, faint bells through a mirror that
faces the wall holding what is new,
what is known
that approaches and passes us.

The Lake: Lise's Wedding

She wakes to a bright fever
of skirts on the lawn, women pulling things
into place. Her father's boats drawn up
off the lake and filled
with bouquets and lanterns are later
allowed to drift out again—
white flowers with lights in a shell
on black water. The gardener's son
will tow them back the next morning.

This day will resist the effects of water
which decorates without request. The girl
pulling back from her window
sheds all pretense of that first scene.
Someone is being undressed in the next room
for a wedding. She imagines something.
What she won't say:

that there's almost no sound to
the twist and curve that strips back
from a green twig. A shove
across the knees and it pulls
apart. Only once
does it hurt. Though,
now, in her left slipper the rim
of a penny is cutting her heel.
She won't touch it, until
tossing those shoes across the floor,
she'll hold the cold coin
to her cheek, her eyes, her mouth.

She is not pretty
or very young, but lovely and
almost invisible at the edge
of the water. A white hat
floats by. There is a stairway

through the trees above her swarming
with violins that trace
her sister's laughter. Everything
teases. The ribbons on the hat
are interesting to a few fish behind
a rock. The water seems solid.

Across the lake a man sitting
on a stone by his garden prepares
a whole trout, with mint
and fresh lemons. He prefers
to eat alone, then fall asleep low
in the September light ignoring
any sound carried on the water.
Death and ceremony are lucid. He won't
attend. It isn't dull
or lonely to wake at dusk and hurl
the thin spine of a fish

over the wall, and smoke while watching
patiently for a yellow moon that's
suddenly confused with four
white globes coming over the water.

Natasha: Portrait Without Landscape

I will fill this grey paper with words
in the calyx light. Outside
you are beating the trees, raising
the clear fluids to restore them
and return all angles to motion.
The air
is full of ashes. I hear the birds lift

out of the branches, their poor nests
shaking and dropping. You
come through the door to tell me
that the leaves have opened
for boiling, that there will be
fresh water. All winter

I have watched a blue insect
in a jar, pacing
his dry ferns. I would wear him,
if he dies, on a thin gold chain
in the evenings. I would dance for you
and learn to be naked

in this odd shelter which frightens me.
There's a return, all light Pierre,
and cadence, that sustains the idea
of showing you everything, outstretched

and tipped
as a single blue wing under glass.

The Family Rostov: New Year's Eve

The visitors
arrive from the silence of their black carriages
into a sudden spill of polished voices,
of skirts spinning in the hallway.
Here, early in the morning,
there were just four children rolling eggs

along the carpet while paper boats,
tied with ribbons, rose in a lacquered vase
in preparation for a story. This story
removes itself and asks even the youngest
to meet these shining, red faced men
and the white shoulders of women stained with pearls
and topaz, those dull jewels
that suck the evening light from chandeliers,
from the bright-eyed children
waiting for dessert. It is lovely

to touch the pistol hidden in a cloak, to
try the Captain's hat.Two girls
whisper and giggle as one ties the other's
loosened sash. *They are ready
for the dancing.*

Later, the boys
climb up the stairs, crawl into their soft
shirts and talk of war, of riding
the perfect horse. They move the lamp
to capture it while the girls,
in their muslin shifts curl by the mirror
and wait, unspeaking, for the face
of a first lover they are sure will be
the last. These girls
are not alike but, this moment, are the same
strained form of a wish in the darkness
reaching beyond the walls and window

out into the thick snow. Who would think
of sleep for them, or any ending to this day,

or any end at all.

CONSENT

Perhaps everyone is still asleep and you,
leaning at the window, watch the violet
shadows thinning on the streets. You'd like
to say that snow clarifies the blood
of that child huddled in a doorway. Today
during this siege it has come to cover him.
His feet and trousers appearing in the Spring.

Someone drunk creeps up the stairs and knows
a stranger's here. Too old for words he falls
asleep behind the wall and we
are safe today while I keep twirling in this blue
silk robe. The huge white flowers stained now
with tea and chocolate and I can taste
how I won't leave you. Completely. Remembering

that last year everything
was as simple as the cruelty of a boy in summer,
who knows the only bait for eels is the
unfledged young of hedgerow birds and steals
them for his night-lines. Always in the morning
finding some accomplice to take him to the river.

SOLILOQUY THAT BEGINS WITH TWO FAMOUS ALCHEMICAL PAINTINGS

1.
Above, the light is more than white,
radiation with a dark center that is
the intelligence of all this. Please walk
with me, now, without any of them. Please
continue yourself as the birds flow
out of darkness to these enormous trees
that stand like weapons by our house.

I want to talk you out of those small accidents
that have nothing to do with listening;
the last defeats you allow yourself, like you, don't mean well.
Once you saw the picture
that could be you tonight: white arms and legs

in different places, the torso
like the chopped center of an egg, and
the head off to one side has your eyes
still open. Beside yourself you stand
with the knife, its two
red edges in the light. Or this—

you've stepped out of a pond and haven't
looked yet at your dripping skin
which is equally black and white. You'd
been swimming a moment ago on a summer day
with old friends and children and have just
passed through the lens into
another picture you must endure, burning

the soft skin to ash while the gravel
and fluid inside you are scattered
to feed the rough, plummeting birds.

2.

The men in the pit have cut open
their arms in the rain. They are adding
their blood to water for bathing
the pigs. This tells you something,
but what—*that it all*
straightens out in another world?
You walk down to join them; the hole
in your arm is putrid,
and they ignore you. You're nobody's
sister at heart; as a daughter you run,

are caught, humiliated. You humiliate,
are cruel with the advantage of beauty
but you're never beautiful, or
might have been once, as a pretty child,
might have been a songbird in winter
that pleased someone, unexpected and simple. . . . .

3.
Do you think *this* matters, that
a construct solves or could force
an honest change? You really are
in love with what they ought to see
in you. All the children
get cookies before they're run off
your false territory. Order
and early sorrow in warm weather.

You are waiting for night
like a staircase, isolated levels
discovered in fog. *Mother*
you want *Queen* and the ability

to dazzle and be believed. *This*
will change nothing; they should have
taken you apart years ago
and started over as with a first

garden being opened. All
the dead materials shoveled in
and used. *Mother*.
there's a sparrow pecking at your fingers.

Be that sparrow. The stairs.

4.
You have painted evening, a sense
of marriage, but not of being *one.*
Just words as you let yourself dissolve
simply in function, *this*, then *this*.

I am the small Nun-bird entering your eyes
with this voice, for the last time,
yourself. In the summer pond
there is the wreckage of a boat
and the feathers of every dead bird.
Underwater, a man and a woman embrace

without breathing. The air above the pond
is all white light and burning,
burning the coldest water to a belief in fire.
The couple is first blue with cold,
then ash-black; they are burning
underwater, under light.
There is no noise as the ashes
heave up out of the pond:

a fountain of white on white
becomes your chance as you hear the fine pulse
hidden in a bird's egg that you must give away.

5.
A family should take its meals together.

Summer, and we are all out on the terrace
at sunset. Thrushes have marked
the first darkness, closed shadows
in the birches by the field. Our daughter
watches her horse nose through the daisies
that are the last whiteness we see at dusk.

I say you have finished a book today
while I was in the garden. I am writing
my book now, slowly, carefully and this house
behind us has new creosoted clapboards
I nailed up myself. I lived here
some summers as a child. Perhaps

my mother is upstairs reading,
a visitor. I remember how pretty
she could be. That's all. This
is now, or a possibility. I am sentimental.

There are even real roses by the wall,
their new air. The birds
have stopped; crickets and the small
brook by the orchard are loud, and louder.
We talk now, without talking.
I have a face I can live with,

and yours, and a strange, beautiful daughter
who just now begins to walk away.
She kisses her horse goodnight before
she leaves with the neighbor's son
to swim with the others at the pond.
There is a moon and I think

a wing just crossed it
out of the woods. It's dark. We're alone
and tired, slowly leaving it all to her.

from *Cascades*, 1979

THE LUMINIST AT AGE ELEVEN

She's heard that apples go silver in moonlight,
that the lavender cloud

of phlox along the wall
is absorbed by rocks, and that even

the steady, village church is eaten away
on a night like this.

They told her when the moon shines
through a stained-glass window, there are no

reds or blues crossing the floor, that
the light is a kind of air. She pictures

her foot lifting and vanishing
through wet grass. *First this,*

then that, depends on seeing and remembering
how it is. If apples

are suddenly falling, then they are solid
when once they were just a thin

scent rising from the fields. So even the best
lit barn is a study in half-tones, and

their opposites. She wonders, how
did they discover lucules, the brighter flecks

at the center of the sun. Could they ever
see just *one* thing again! Could that person,

who no longer has to imagine *universe*
and *source*, come back to paint the north side

of a wooden house. All this like
someone waking in the dark. The strands

of light under her door are a lamp left on
by the man and woman talking in the next room.

They sigh at the contrariness of children
while outside, down the lane, the sickle moon

has just stopped beyond the orchard.

ROUTE 116 TO CONWAY

A road that becomes smaller
as it lifts further away from the sea, west
into the hills. This tar,
heavily shaded to green and black shadows,

is printed in memory
as the way out of the city, its heat—
away from towns
to my grandfather's house: stained
clapboards, surrounded by fields
where I would trample a maze
with walls of hay that breathed.

I'd lie in the hot, backseat
of the Plymouth dreaming the car
leaped over each shadow
that crossed my cheek—from
air to pavement to air again! We'd
get there faster. One August morning

I sat up, sick from the drive,
and saw them on the long,
curved bank of the Mill River: *six
little people, their house and barn,
two dogs and a cow.* They waved
at me as surely as this white page
accepts ink. No one

believed me. Twenty years later I see
the people each day
while driving back from work.
I see them waving across fast water,
across icy banks in winter.
They speak of traveling that road
with its fragments of blue sky,
patches of air. It takes me,

always tugging back from nausea,
through the teasing maples, my shadow
behind the wheel tracking voices
that croon the horizontal ease of a larger,
darker welcoming among tall grass and leaves.

AUTOPSY

When you are tired of this bread and salt
you'll be tired of one another.
—From a Gypsy wedding ceremony

Vaya's never hungry anymore, just a little salt
in beer. Saviya's working in a store,
a gossip with crepe-soled shoes, her arms
bloodless by night. She's cruel

and likes to flirt, flirt
because she isn't pretty in the mornings
with her tangled hair. She drinks
and giggles to a flush, her red

awkward fingers slipping needles
through a skirt she needs to wear at work.
The sky boils, cloud
on darker cloud while Vaya, huddled

by the birch tree, shivers his fear of rain.
They'd told him of the old ways, of the day
his grandmother died in childbirth
on a mattress in a field. How two fresh eggs

were placed beneath her arms to keep
vampires from drawing off her milk.
He thinks he hates his wife who washes
sorrel in the sink. He wishes

she had yellow hair and spoke
more softly. He knows himself to be
divorced from water. In his pocket,
three bird skulls he says

belong to magpies. He binds them

with thread and sprigs of rosemary
to an ornament he'll place beneath her head.
If her sleep's disturbed

she's unfaithful, the nightmare rising
like a pattern of ferns above the bed,
each frond a knife scratching
a lover's name because in daytime life she cannot say:

> *we watched the water flush like rootless hair*
> *across the rocks at Chapel Falls, saw the forest*
> *like our own skins peeled back.*
> *Husband, you forgot me for a tin guitar—*
>
> *its strap my golden wedding necklace*
> *rattling against painted tin. Now the clatter*
> *of magpies peck at my sleep incessant*
> *as the rain you hate,*
> *smoking all the windows of our dreams.*

ABOVE THE TOBACCO FIELDS OF SOUTH DEERFIELD, MASSACHUSETTS

for the Orlens

This is only a small mountain under
the breathy pines, but below us, the spellbinding
nets heave above tobacco: creamy shades
trailing the dark borders of trees and water.
From here the gauze

seems a fog cheating my sense
of solid ground, but attractive like a soft
conclusion of sleep. Since I was young,
I've been transfixed by looking down
on this mysterious shuddering
across the valley. I think it's always
defined the helplessness of distance,
of life frail as the green wrapper-leaves

that later this summer will hang in airy barns
then dry to tough, brown papers.
Beyond this clearing, in '65, Miss Alaska
lost her footing and fell
to the stumpy field near the river. Her skirt
and up-flung arms sparking
like bridal flowers, she landed far beyond
any outstretched hands. She must
have trusted in reaching the nets
and sliding down that moth-colored
map all the way to the sea.

Today is just another summer picnic;
I let the strawberries roll into dirt and look down
to the clouded margins of the river
where I could wind myself through passages
of broad, young leaves as hopeless
of change as a bitter taste—

but pleased all the same by the milky-cloth
ceiling that extends
the comfort of evening in a summer breeze.

VIGIL

The household grows obscene
next to red petals on the floor.
Who will bother
to pick them up, silky and pungent
in the hand, the hand
at the red mouth closing? Together
the woman and the flower
suffer a secret disturbance.

In the hallway, a lamp
glows thinly through the front window
to deceive everyone
coming back from the fields
and barns. The gears

in the standing clock have
brass teeth that squeak *our heart
is stopping.* In the cellar,
onions are in bed with straw
and potatoes. Upstairs, a carpet
of painted husks covers
the wall, tapestry that lilts
then settles like clouds
losing substance in the trees. This signal

recalls the waxy, red hand of her grandfather
who was once a boy being pulled
from a burning stable by a servant
just his age. The war in her mind
gives up to a life like a bird dividing itself
in reflection. Those small wings which reach

for both water and the sky.

FOR FEBRUARY'S DARK SIMPLE

Prepared by conversations—
you're never prepared. You know,
hearing the rain break up in syllables,
that the broken speech of adults
has finally deceived you. We could never
tell you how the largest truths
come in another language, how this
familiar room clenching blue around you
would be full of strangers. Your father
and I, and a neighbor. Your two small fists
are part of your face; they keep us out!

Someone you met at the neighbor's house
routed a slow death like complicated wires
through his body. You see him go from
rose to grey on hospital sheets and imagine
the cut flowers taking your complexion
for themselves. You said,

Mr. O. has got a coma and began to cry!

I say, think of the soft cloud he's swallowed now
that will lift him from inside-out, think
how he's left his long, white board
for a gentle net like any
yellow, autumn hammock. Think of
anything but this, think of nothing

because nothing works; I try to touch your shoulder,
hair, try to wipe your face with water
cooler than tears. The senses, here,
refuse mothering and I feel criminal
with sweet-talk. How, all these years,

tucking the quilt around you
was a white lie, how the largest feelings

force us to know we're really all alone.
Even now, while the desert
that circles this town is eating rain,
it's terrible rim of mountains can shoot
to color. You're eight years old, curled up
in a gold chair, furious
and sad at all the sadness even as
we bring it on ourselves. The air you feel
stretches beyond these walls where we
seem placed like miniature prophets and
your tears run hot, then chill—because

even as we love you, we knew nothing first.

THE PEARS

And the pears were useless and soft
Like used hopes, under the starlight's
Small knowledge . . . .
—Delmore Schwartz

At noon wasps clink and whirr
under the pear tree like bits
of brown and yellow fruit rising sharply
back into the leaves; they
dive again where the soft pears
flatten in the grass. It's late September

and the whole garden is giving up
to a grey collapse while I cut the last
green tomatoes with their rust spots; they join
the garlic, celery and dill in clear jars
I fill with vinegar. Our father

is dead, having sickened faster than the small
plot of vegetables I raised in this gritty
New England soil. A sudden
wing drooped from his body while the three
of you stood by, believing in his death
as your private shadow. He never told you

he married a girl from Boston at nineteen
who he didn't see again after
she had given birth to me one winter morning.
But I grew up knowing of you, your faces
nearly Asian like your mother's,
and wondering
if just one of our features
were the same, perhaps his unmistakable
eyebrows. I can smell
the fallen pears from the window,
even stronger in the evening now, damp

and sweet as fresh cake.
The wasps are sleeping
in the eaves. It's cooler and in just
weeks clouds of grosbeaks
will start descending, morning and night,
to feed in the yard, in the broken sticks
of the garden. The pears

will have melted by the roots of their tree
as though they never existed, even in the memory
of chilly wasps, fat and dying
in grey paper nests. You have buried
our father out where it's always summer
near a garden of keyaki, pink lotus and jasmine. Perhaps,
you've finally learned of me, the facts of death
not included in his life. You might think of me, then,
as a blonde working in a dress-store—as impossible

as halves of a pear—left out
to be shared
by an odd number of difficult children.

CASCADES

for Norman

I
perihelion

The blue rocking chair recedes at dusk, becomes
nearly colorless, but the child
still says *blue* and *sky,* climbs up, and pointing
at the tacks along the edge, says *stars*
to fall asleep. The chair's small motion
pulls her closer to the center of the room. She thinks
she's sleeping in the sky, cradled
in a dark nebula, and when she shifts around—
the occultation of a thousand stars inside me.

We're hand in hand
as children are in all of us, binaries
swinging from *curious* to *absolute*
and back again beyond
our mutual distrust, a pure point
that's ephemeral and radiant
in whatever we imagine
has invented us. The shadow

of the trellis on the lawn stretches
like a girl with extended arms. With one leg
straight, and then the other, she reaches
for everything in all directions
throughout the day. But we outgrow

this horizontal sweep by paying close attention
to our lives. Our first
solution is the sun. The asters
opening on the hillside are a deep,
central lavender, an enticement
to gather what we see

in a loose arrangement while our poor bodies
strike an eclipse.
A red leaf smacks into the drainpipe
and flushes down along the path. Its soft
luminosity in grey weather startles
today. Next spring, we'll notice green.
In summer, the grapes
clustering at the trellis edge,
will seem sprayed by a surprising mist
that a finger wipes away. You want

your shoes repaired and our child's just
turned twelve. How much we've lived
through—worn down shoes and old
iron skillets hanging on the wall.
The wall itself has stood two hundred years,

the pans fashioned from the same
element that, white-hot, crashed
down from the sky destroying
a herd of reindeer and acres of trees
one Siberian winter. The man
who saw it fall believed he was on fire.
He shook in his sleep for seven months,
and then one morning walked down into the river.

We know each other, and a few
other things, and part of our daughter
who's up in the wet maple tree. She's moving
from curious to absolute, to wherever
it takes her, higher

than all the branches and beyond the rain.

II

aphelion

The rain is coming harder over the spiked
blue spruce; it aims at you. You run
from the garden to the shed, tumbling
hoe and trowel. You run
slower than the rain up to the porch.
There's thunder crawling off the lake,
the screens puff inward and the late roses
are whirling, disturbed. Fierce water

playing on the roof reminds us
of the desert when tall palms
lashed out in dust storms. Then,
they reminded us of home,
of rain on a hot barn
some August evenings. We are always
sick for an opposite, for what
was *new.* But every fresh memory
is new and shared like this odd, Chinese
carpet at the foot of the stairs—
a remnant from another life,
pearl-grey and blue tradition

of leaves, water, air!

III.

black hole

We don't walk in the field at night.
The scare surrounds us as we're drawn down
on the wet grass by each other, by it.
Pale flowers brush my arms, my hair
feathers to a net. You
are my heavy occultation as one by one
every visible thing goes out.
Its own failure to defeat you falls in on itself,
a chaos drawing everything inward, and there is such pull
that no light escapes. This absence

is a flower swallowing all
its seeds, a leaf eaten by a twig,
this *nothing* so solidly itself appears
as a passage, a tunnel
between worlds. We could curl up
and roll through to a further
light beyond. There's no way

to see it, a complete wall
of heat, a necklace which embraces
all our galaxies—

its clasp a black pearl on the body
of a dream
that dreamt of us, at the beginning.

IV

the parallax

She is making her mouth red,
though in moonlight, it will look
pure black. She's fourteen. All music

plays just for her. A blue shirt
shows her off
blonder than she is and she believes

she's ready for anything. In the rill
beside the stream, all the apple trees
are letting go in bloom. *Cascades*
is the password, and she is over the sill,
outside at night. The maple trees
are fainter than their shadows. This escape

across the field is cinematic, backed
by the starry windows of the town, its one
steeple pointing like Draco's tongue

toward the large, cold moon playing light
off the farmhouse. *This is the night
of the first time.* She makes it up

as she remembers her short amazement
at the black spots of blood along her leg.
The blur, the roots against her spine

and a few scrapes. This was being third person
as she saw herself give up, anecdote
to her traveling beneath pink flowers.
She saw the moon assume mortality and stop
perfectly on her face. Poor us, she thought,

and all the physical world stood up!

V

On an ordinary autumn night, Tycho Brahe
was struck by surprise. He said
nova and, meaning it, named
a sudden brightness that could be seen
in daylight, or through
the thickest clouds at night. *Nova,*

our ability to name
simply as we do the unborn.
The parts we know we keep, those small faces
beyond ourselves. We believe that space

goes on. The older we become
the more our eyes are hopeful
for the twin-self staring back
from the Magellanic Clouds, their capture
in the mind where children
grow black radishes under a redder sky.

Tonight, just the leaves are red
in darkening rain. No moon
or stars can penetrate that curtain
as we settle in our chairs.
There's no one else
but us, though once our curtain
opened on a larger world.
I think I'm fresher now
than that sprawling girl;
I've come alive, dreaming
of what dreamed us first, naming

what we share: this constellation
that is ourselves crossing the room
from chair to blue rocker,
slow shifting along a surface to a space—

night and day. Day and night

from *Silentia Lunae*, 1981

"Day by day new mercies unfold"—Robert Chelsea

SILENTIA LUNAE

Beyond the orchard and its blue hushed
hillside is the river I get to
by repeating your name three times and taking
the sunless passage behind my eyes
down to patient water. The trees twist

behind me, saddened it seems, by their roots
and stillness. They wish for the trilled
piping of birds, a lullaby of leaf
brushing leaf above rocks, the wind . . . .
But on days like today, when I lose
that name, the blue beads
I was weaving into my hair vanish
as the blank doorway
spills you home again, hungry.

*

I know how ghosts have sealed
your eyes; it's true they are
transparent and you still see
beyond their silken breath. But once
touched by it, the boundary softens
and the line you thought you could not cross
becomes witness to your trust. To ours.

There's a man in me just shifting
out of boyhood. He talks slyly
to other boys, draping slender fingers
seriously on their wrists. For months,
he simply vanishes into someone else's air
always returning nameless with the night.

*

Prone across the footbridge, you trail
your hand through sluggish water
and name each leaf
floating past you toward the river.

Pegasus, Sabha, Eclipse:
eyes closed, you ride them all the way
to the sea and back to this solitary stream
your father named as *yours*. Dear Twin,

though we're always out of step,
I'm grateful that our eyes
can see beyond their ridge of bone
into the vortex of the grave and up

where trees lift their tongue and veins
through the swept air. And we, earthbound still,
keep searching upturned, unsure.

        One of us is always
above water staring down, the other
weighted into its bed, looks up. How we change,
and why, we cannot know, only that it happens, that
we share a binary mirror.

It's my turn now to see you
luminous through this watery lens,
your dark circle of hair,

eyes like washed stones. I lie here
with leaves passing above my open eyes, a few
black twigs distorting you
as you watch your *other* bloom
like a paper flower. The stream

drags off my clothes one by one, torn
petals that you touch

as they go by. I have no name for you,
male moon of myself, though reaching farther
you almost touch me with desire.

*

The stream pulls itself to Chapel Falls, down
the moss-lined granite walls, over black
swollen logs, lichen-paled and wedged
to softness in constant water. By now,
the rutilant leaves must be quilting all
the fields' perimeters. I'd walk there with you

burying the garden's dead—a ceremony
of purpose—before snow stiffens the ground
and hides it from us. I'd take the path
along the falls to watch smaller leaves
spin down to darkening pools. There,
like cat-yellow eyes, they spiral almost
to stillness, staring at the thinned out sky.
I reach to catch the brightest, speckled

eye and bring it to my mouth—*where are you*?
I paste it to my cheek and walk uphill
toward gravel, asphalt, and the power lines
humming light from town to town. I know
how the certain dead pull me down, leveled
and bring me back to you

with words and a single shining leaf and mouth.

CRIME & PUNISHMENT

The water is rising & time moves sideways again:
my ribcage is a jar, it's lip my throat
as water tumbles against the narrowing
aperture. How close it comes. After all,
it was bloodless until now; the anarchist,
with his loop of piano wire running just one
red seam across the clouds, was hardly believable.
I will not go out again, denying nothing. Long
blue shadows cross the hillside, seeping
closer. The water is hurting, forced
to be a boundary between the victim
& his blood. If he bleeds underwater
we will never know it happened until
that water evaporates, falling again
over the shadowed hills like a red
& final metamorphic snow. Last time,
I put the corpse in a suitable garden;
springtime flourished & I veiled myself
in lacy hysteria tricking the flowers
into bloom. This is not different
until it is. My great-grandmother's bequest?
A necklace of tiny jeweled skulls, for each
a jar of seawater buried in the yard. The problem was
the original story. I should have
laughed it off, but was enthralled instead.
Cover this one with your breath & he
will find you; paste this one to your inner thigh
to protect you from disease; the green-eyed one
for unlikely luck; & this? Keep against your throat
to stop the water rising. Beware
of others like ourselves
& always keep these hidden. But I am lying again.
I forged the chain myself from the gulley
of a dream. It was filling with water & maybe
the chain of skulls pulled me in; I am still paying.
I think I must be stopped before the animals

come to drink at dusk. They should have *clear*
water & so should you & the children. I think
the jar must be broken & then a ribbon
placed around my throat to hide that red
wire mark emerging now from years ago.

APRICOTS

Early-ripe, those haunches spin
below lacquered green leaves.
When you touch one, the motionless
gold air is stirred
to a penumbra throbbing in your hand.
Its softness deceives you; it
barely bruises but when it does
paler spots emerge.
          You think back
to that shift of sun dappling
her cheek—irregular
ancient coins—behind shutters
closed on the afternoon. A small
burning orb swivels in your palm.
You close around it and remember
Arthur in his Great Hall, fearful
of dominion, of the fractured
angle of brotherhood, and of woman.
          But she,
turning down the sheet, shines
beneath watery green shadows.
In a bowl, the yellow fruit
are what they seem in this world
that sometimes tilts furiously
behind your eyes. She lifts
her arm which just curves
harmlessly. This radiance is
purer than blood
feathering desire. You're drawn closer,
and what you reach for
sighs and goes for your mouth:
little cleft of sunlight
          attainable
touching gently
the corridors deep in a stone castle.

EURYDICE

I molt in the face.
The lake's skin
toughens this summer.

Yellow chintz hangs in the window.
Water pulls along my eyes
yet you stand nearby
where I am not in love, and

fire's in the lake, paper boats
sail off the island's lip.
I lived there once
as air above the flames.

There are times a man's torso
in the concave clench of love,
makes an animal face.
At those moments

I want to send you a postcard
saying *slow dance, dusk
thunder over trees,* saying

I am not air. I am just
not. Lift your head
and reach for me across the world.

Shouts from the island, tall pines
and a clearing where blueberries ripen
from their blood color of someone stabbed yesterday.

The boats have caught fire, cannot
live in water. An edge
of yellow in my mouth, I bite down hard.
That face surging in window glass,
is it mine? Someone's opening the door

and I won't look.

OF MY FATHER

A child flings herself into those pine woods
where blue jays snap the air in half.
Blood-trillium reduce the shade of earth
unpatching from snow. I am back

in that instant I misplaced years ago
leading to a summer pond called evening, home.

There's the corpse with countless faces
rising from water. He calls me toward his gifts
scattered among far trees: terms
of endearment, thin lips and the lilting
gold chain that locks down my throat.

I have always worn it.

Two or three women pulse in the radius of my wrist.
Cassandra, Marie, and delicate Anne.
None of them are me.
I wake from this—a self torn from others
who, if she had her way,
would be rinsing her arms and legs
in the moon's deft, predictable light.

But it's nearly dawn. A first bird unlatches.

The man beside me sleeps with his long legs walking away.
His eyes open briefly. I lean above him
and see how he holds back the enveloping breath,
seeing also how deeply he could give it.
I kiss his shoulder

and what I say no one hears

as the gold scar on my neck breaks and the forest
falls toward me: blood—

lover of night face down in water
the wildflowers want gathering.
The name is in my mouth and I'm not able.

PROTHALAMIUM

They've thrown us in jail:
me inside the walls,
you outside.
—Nazim Hikmet

I have opened the door; there's a wind outside
that changes everything. I might be home
by a pond at dusk, the sharp
rain-scented wind rising to stir the water,
and my hair. This is the first breath
of autumn in the desert. My cat bathes
in the window-air as mulberry trees
toss into darkness. This wind holds
the wordlessness of beginning again. A gesture
that faces into it through sleep.
I am certain only that the cat stretches,
feeling all of herself, and that my hand
is here, yours, somewhere else. All of this
because the wind reminds me of home
and of a pond I might show you where the same wind
finds us walking, uncovered by rain.

*

Didn't we once ride horses together?
There was a hayloft's secrecy, the vacant
air we swam through, uncut fields
trampled to mazes. We shared those rooms,
the jack knife and contraband Luckies in childhood's
alliance. Here, in the Visiting Room, our eyes
meet, slide, meet again. And they foolishly
call us *lovers* . . . .

The pond has opened its eye to summer. Weeds
at the edge darken their green. They stir;
tree frogs are blending their songs

for tonight, just tonight, and there
are the fireflies I always promised you.
How that senseless desert heat
held nothing like home, but this field
rimmed with birches has gone dark as the pond:
an eye widened to take both our bodies in.
How pale we are at dusk, your leg stretched
all the way along mine
under this spring-fed northern water.

*

I used to sleep in a house guarded
by a wall of pines. They loosened snow
from their dark centers. It piled
onto the steps and sills. On a mountain
I own in my mind, snow blurs everything now.
Your face flickers through the dense
white. Breaking through that opaque cold,
I see iron gates close hard
behind you. Your shoulders gone into a blizzard
beyond my reach. I dress for winter,
a vigil that will seem forever. See, there I am
in a red cap and jacket. Like the hunter
who's left his gun at home, I wait
to see just how thick the snow falls
and what stranger will walk vividly out of it.

Remember, you dreamt of the room? Its
table and chairs, two windows. Here's
something that resembles it. Behind my eyes
are yours: pine boards, resin-dark, the white
quilt bunched in a corner. Like flying,
our arms rise and fall
to spread out the bedding. Shoes
abandoned, your hands press
at the window as a thrush brings round
our first evening home. The purple lid

of sunset dimming behind the ridge.
I told you it would be like this, once
at least! And now you look hard into my face
for the mirror I carry—its infinite
silver passage that we carefully tend

despite the fat,
brown-shirted man who taps your shoulder again . . . .

for M.

from *Nightblind*, 1985

THE WIND OF LATE SUMMER

At first, what flew hard from my grandfather's mouth
into my mother's ribs was a feeling,
no more, no less.
Call it anger, call it love,
call it thunder cracking against the pines.

She never spoke of that moon looking up from the lake,
or the loons with their terrible noise.
The doorknob turned. His hands
became two red knots slipping at her breasts
while the wind rose on its hind legs.

Don't tell me I can't speak of this. My mother
hummed in her sleep as the mist off Sebago
sucked all light from the windows.
Grandfather stomped through the house
like it was still outdoors.

My mother wakes now over and over
to rattle about in the kitchen. She never thinks
of those sheets once pale beneath her storm-bound hair.
The house still stands in its timber.
It's August again, and wind brushes the pines

with the blurred sound of a girl's dress, torn
and falling. But Mother doesn't listen.

SPRING

The scent is back, a bridal weave
across the city. All night
the kiss won't leave our mouths
and memory steps, with dark measure,
between us and the flowers.

If we rise to this, the white
budded stars will shake,
the sky fall back to air.
I know what I've worn in my bones since birth,
hands at my throat, hands
at my knees, that swift red stain
between my teeth.

The future of memory flares.
We age, the flowers return. The trees I pass each day
fill up with birds. I pick
a single orange blossom which I crush to my wrist.

I could rub its skin to music, break
a man's bones to get to the heart.
I have only
one slow breath riveted to breath—

the stars stammer back their light
oil of flowers, bright enemy, heart.

A FORMAL PROBLEM

A wish makes up their dream
until the dream's long conversation
reshapes that wish. But this diversion
of husband and wife
is a mutual child pulling back the sheets
until its parents say
"what have we made
from all this toss and fall—
is this really what, and where, we'll stay?"

Night to night, they sleep
kept from day's toughening light
until they separate in relief
and dreams walk back
into wishing's first need:
a man tending to his job, a woman
to her house, both to the small
gleaming hedges and walls
that daily bank their bodies in.

What is it, then, that begins to stir
as mortal dreaming comes apart?
In that white solid bed he touches
her slow thighs just to lose
her face and name, while she
lies in the crooked latch of his arms,
afraid her last wish—that he might die—
shines out, blank as prayer,
from her damp undreaming eyes.

ORPHEUS TRANSPOSED AMONG THE WILLOWS

Here now they walk together side by side,
Sometimes he follows her as she proceeds,
Sometimes he goes ahead and safely now
Looks back at his Eurydice.
—Ovid

Orpheus dreams of willows draping the river
by that meadow where she died. How she gasped
with surprise, serpent teeth flashing
in the veins behind her knee.
Between worlds, she just looks at him. He wakes

as a severed thigh sings the blood-light
of an artery, its split
pomegranate of the many and one. Seeds
scrape his tongue. He hears her call him back,
for in between his world and hers
she has no dominion. Rising once,
she opens wide her arms as the wind
throws itself from all directions

and she is driven down to that waiting room
where she sits
smoothing her skirt around two good legs.

*

Unlocking his throat, Orpheus stands
at his window and sees how the trees
beckon. Willow spikes are notation
against the sky. They teach him
all they know of exile: the speech
of animals and the one, many-sided song
no woman can resist. He knows
how she'll elude him if the words
go wrong, but trusts

the history of lyric far better
than her kiss. Even as she turns towards him
out of darkness, he cannot see
the soft trees falling through the mirror
of her weighted eyes.
The trees are full of love and from the deep
center of her reflection
she cannot believe his arms forget her,

cannot bear the dusky waiting much longer.

*

He washes his face in brackish water,
pulls tight his belt, rolls his sleeves
down against the chill. He whistles
and thinks of how he'll try for her
though he has no knife against the gods.
The throat of Orpheus is steep, walls
close in and what's lyric
has lost its melody of light. He can't
make out the gate until, suddenly,
like stars surging, he sees
her white knees shine. Those thighs
and two covered breasts he must not yet touch.
A shadow falls across his eyes
so he can't see her as she is, or imagine
what will be if they make it back alive.

*

He has found the word to keep a single
threaded note glowing in ascent. He thinks
again of willows, branch kissing slow
branch above restless water. But she's humming
beneath her breath. The air behind him
brushes up against his neck. *Would she dare*

touch him just to die again? He fears her,
for her, and who they are. They have sworn again
to release that death-star that's pulsed
for centuries inside their mouths.

Fists deep in his pockets, Orpheus walks, singing
so he cannot hear her, shrugs off
those long fingers at his nape, her gaze
burning between his shoulders. The song
pitches higher, weaves the world
inside-and-out to one note
that cannot tear. It seems *forever.*
His feet are stones, many and one; he sees
not moon, but a flaming cleft between boulders.
She claws his back, begs
that if he loves her now, to look! There

the river. Its signature catching sun!
Willows scrape the earth. He leans
across the bank that no longer
laments, sees above his watery face
her two eyes staring, silver, up at him.
Turning with a first awkward kiss, he takes
from between her lips that coin-cold star
and spits it into Lethe
it flickers, sinks, and they walk home
together, safe beyond the shade of willows—
across the meadow
each deep in the shade of the other's world.

HURT ISLAND

One house
is halfway up a hill.
A pocked August sun
suppurates
unkindly at the sill.

Beneath the stairs,
a child sways
humming, humming
while Father's face,
pummeled as damp new clay,

empties its blue
into an emptier day.
Whoever his wife is
leans at pots and pans.
She wears stained brown hands

difficult to kiss
and her knees scrape dry,
gristle to bone.
But tip to toe,
the specific child

goes twirling down the hall.
Against her chest,
a red rag doll.
She knows the world
is full of steam,

that it smells of chicken,
onions, greens,
that nothing shines
but the teething sea.
Above long tall dunes, clouds

extend their fish-spot hides.
This one day is always
a dank ancestral song:
Sunday's swollen liver
and all the house gone wrong.

NIGHTBLIND

When that train's headlight veers
to kill my right eye, I panic
and the road goes black.
There are no white-line boundaries.
The radio croons *I can't*
stop loving you so I ask
each truck that passes to rescue me
back on course.

Aiming for their small red lights,
I name the drivers: Texas John
with a load of drills, Norman out of Tulsa
for Safeway again, and hailing
mud-splattered from Florida
is Skinny Bill "Truckin' for Jesus."

If I sit beside him high up in the cab,
he tells me he's moving pom-poms and batons,
and that it's God's will you're gone.
Then he lists the ways I should repent:
ashes, denial, prayer. Recalling
the brightness of your hand across my leg,
I can only say there's not one bit of evidence
I ever knew you. No bruises,
no address, no fallen threads of hair.

Steering by instinct, I get to that blank stretch
where mountains flatten
and stars pitch white along their edge.
I feel stupid with your name in my mouth,
or to claim that what's not seen
is even there. So stupid
that what I touched
was just loneliness crouched beneath your ribs
striking blindly out, within my arms

POSTCARD

Dusk, the sea is between colors
and our medallion star is ready to leave for China.
This is the brushstroke hour
you have already befriended.

I am here for the first time
taking a rush of water into my mouth.
My ribs fold with a white salt weight.

Centuries ago, Mu Ch'i slipped his eye
from fog to indigo. A grain of sand
dislodged from a monastery wall.

His six bitter orbs of fruit
are still blindingly pure,
and everyday
his seventh, unpainted persimmon
ripens across the sky.

The bell-blossom moon follows behind.

Here, in California, the day shakes once
and falls. The ocean pulls closer.
With luck, you say,
a sudden streak will flash toward the stars

as the flaming persimmon dips into salt.

In this way the eye will complete the day.
It will root in the heart.
My hands return from water, the water
returns from China.

I would unstain my heart to carry it with me.

CUP & SAUCER

For Becky Roach

Little flat water, little
water that pretends it isn't the sea.
Clear, just dusted water
in its tea-set sibling shapes.
The trackless sand settles.
This is where children find private season
between fallen primrose
& the blackberries' white
cut-out stars. This is where
limpet shells hold fast
& the water is warm. Basket & towel
are tossed away while, naked,
a girl stretches her first body out
& grins to be the Saucer's spoon.
In the Cup, a boy jumps up & down
shouting all of himself for her.
Sometimes they splash each other
to salted bloom, or chase
a lucky stone toward ferns. Here,
at low tide, these pools keep house
for children, but
in harder weather repair to sea.
As the children grow, their arms & legs
must buckle to fit
so they move to other summer things.
The girl, fiery & dark, now
fashions tarts & cakes. The boy
works hard his boat while water
waits all of its seasons.
Tourists swarm the cliff path, dogs
clatter about to piss
& there are fewer water-skinned children
for this place. Genderless as memory,
the worn shapes remain

half-used, the way a man & woman late for work
leave dishes on the table. What spills
is a little water, twin
to little flat water waiting for the sea.

from *Infrequent Mysteries*, 1991

FICTION'S DAUGHTER

I eat myself a family: each quart of ice cream, a tidy
blonde Mom in shirtwaist and pearls crossing the lawn
with a pitcher of fresh lemonade. When she bakes
my whole house smells like paradise. I dream each slab
of chocolate is a perfect Dad in thin important suits
calling *Honey, I'm home!* at 5:25 p.m. precisely.
Me and Little Sister (whose name I can't decide) tumble
into his hugs. My sister likes for me to brush
her hair, weave ribbons through her toes. She's
those boxes of crackers I consume, brisk and gold.

For Christmas I eat cookies and hunks of cheese until my red
velvet stocking hangs beside a *real* fire and I hear
a world full of chimes, not the constant clack of typing.
You'd think knowing all this I would stop,
but I'm someone else's story. My dark, word-
drunk father hardly eats at all. He looms over his book and papers,
then later gently blows a goodnight kiss.
But I'm not safe for sleep unless I'll wake tall,
gorgeous, and thin! Sure,

I have the right long bones, am dusky and pretty
like my first mother. I wear her fire and the red mouth
of her wine stained lips. But she left, and I am left
wide-hipped, built too big for any love to hold.
My first protection is the finger down my throat. Two
step-mothers later, there's less of me. I'd hoped those Moms
would dress for dinner, fuss prettily about a pretty house.
I'd hoped we'd all sit down together. I still long for
that white canopy-bed I saw in a picture when I was five.
I hate boring rooms where only books, and Dad, remain the same.

Those bad-girl nights when biscuits break up in my hands,
I hear the sound of Little Sister's feet brushing
beside me on the way to school. I can't stop
filling myself with those t.v. dreams of family. I'm told

I'm self-destructive—what do they expect—these artists
who made me wrong? With each wrench, each stomach heave
and lash of sweat I try to start again, twist back to zero.
One night I'll float downstairs into the warm
red arms of Santa Claus, into a home where nothing's
criminal and my whole body fills with inhabitant love.

GOOD FRIDAY

The city readies itself for Easter hymns
and cocaine. Leaves flail
in unseasonable wind and red, pink, yellow
petals scatter across indifferent lawns
on this day I no longer love you.

There was a woman I knew who broke her body
into the sea. Her blood swiftly left
the shoreline and took on the no-color of wind.
Once she'd been a flower, a bride
who capped her long dark hair with a veil
and smiled for a man.
Inside, she was very serious and looked away.

I remember how she laughed and smoked,
the cold slippery bottles of milk
in the crook of her arm as she swung herself
up the street each morning. She is why, now,

in a city far away I say no to myself
as I think of you and those terrible words
you'd cry: *What are we going to do! What,
what shall we do?* I think of how that woman
answered herself, and how it felt
when I refused to answer you.

The air is bright today. A calico cat
crouches on the sill while birds
inhabit the sudden gusts above their nests
and my blood calms. I want forgiveness,
and to speak my gratitude for small
easeful things: coffee, phone calls, sauce
on the stove. The precision
of my existence no longer touches you.
For all the living, I pray that *what
shall we do?* be lifted away

as our blood and bodies begin to revive—
when no longer loving
is to love again, and survive.

ON TRANSLATION

The man who scrubs
wipes out the ashtrays one by one
but his wife's
half-filled cup of water
remains smudged
beside her incessant pile of books.

In the passage, a photograph of their child
grins like a candle on this windy night.
The severe white paint
bears no fingerprints.

What accuracies!
The moon drags the harbor deeper and deeper.
They have lived together in such a way
they are beyond wounding one another.

DOGS

Whose roses are being torn apart
by wind and black abrasive rains?
They fall together, thorns
piercing petal and stems
as though a herd of schoolgirls
had maddened in a sewing room
threading thumb to cheek,
torso to thigh. Little girls
caught by wind's heedless desire
slashing across the lawn.

       Another small girl walks to the store with
       two nickels and a dime. Coming home, she stops
       to poke hello at the wrong dog. He sinks
       his teeth hard into her hand. Her mother panics;
       no policeman can find this dog. After yelling,
       the mother lets the child put iodine on the hand
       herself. It colors to rust. Her tears hurt too,
       but going to the doctor is a big white blank.
       Something with eyes from the ceiling watches as
       they hold the child down and needles ease into
       her smooth white abdomen. Something watches
       like a big window or a piece of fire falling
       across her.

The slightest shift of stone,
the smallest sound, prepare
catastrophe for two
speckled eggs resting on the sill.
No bird comes to claim them.

       She remembers the little plaid jacket she wore,
       and the few streaks of blood she carried home.
       She feels her sticky rusted fingers, and the
       policeman's breath close to her face. The rest

is impossible except for black winds, the cross-
hatched rain, a needle's eye? Her mother's open mouth.

Some evenings, God stays
in the sunset above the field
and trees. He plays
the two-pronged song of the phoebe,
or shades that painting
of blue deer leaping a canyon
pinned above her bed. Sometimes
he's Mother humming in the bath.

    But who fills up the night
    with those black dogs
    lifting her hand away
    between their teeth? That hand,
    and the rest of her, pulled
    into thickets or deep
    below the dark brown pond
    where lily pads
    float above her head?

On the lawn, those roses
stay undone—yellow and pink
flattened in mud, thorns
gone soft, leaves
curled up—all flung down
like dresses after a dance.

    Little stones in the stream nearby
    get pushed from their shallow nests
    by tawny rushed waters.
    Twilight falls thin as silk
    above the phoebe and a sudden
    thrush. The field beyond
    seeps toward the last gleam
    from the birches where a doe

steps out to graze. God sleeps
in two eggs on the sill
where the child leans on her elbows
to stare into the ceiling sky
which is not blank
but punctured by stars. Poor big sky
chewed rough at its edges by branches
and leaves. A voice calls from the bottom of the stairs.
dreams click awake
testing their teeth on the rafters.

THE MEADOW

The man with a thick black beard is picture-
framed by sky and trees. His shirt is blue.
Sleeves rolled, he bends into tall feathery grasses,
fingers choosing a shimmer of flowers
as part of the ritual for his child. That's how
the daughter must invent this man who never
sang, or brushed back her hair on any feverish night.
It doesn't matter. The meadow shines. Yellow, white,
orange and blue wildflowers fleck the surface of its world.
The bouquet trembles. The story of its gathering
began the moment that her father shut the door
behind him and vanished towards another life.
She never saw his eyes. As she grew
she chose his face and open arms as though absence
were not her fault, or even his. Years
and years now—the texture of objects, the damp
skin of husbands, the shifting colors of all cats
who've ever needed her have proved the father
will not come back. Still, a child in red sweater
and boots keeps running towards that figure
crouched and bearded in tall grass. He lifts
his arms, beckons and she steps high, again
and again delighted, as long as the meadow lasts.

AT THE HIGH-WATER MARK

I pluck a gull's breastbone away from feathers and weed.
Poor bird, brought in by water–
its white cartilage has the shape of a mouth
open for inspiration, or flight.

I watch the white glaze of bad weather cool against the sky
like a cheap under-slip through which shines
the sun's eye, briefly. I've never liked this dead
height of summer which presses at windows with its long hours.

There's a man not far from here whose blindness
is pale as daytime fog. At least he's not
a child caught in darkness beneath the stairs.
His life is courageous, his bright bandage almost heavenly.

Perhaps that gull slammed first into the sun before it broke apart
leaving something for my fingers to snap off in sand.
The glare from water, that slide of air nagging
at my eyes, makes my body falter.

This wishbone in my hand is as light as the almost-
nothing of a prayer.

INFREQUENT MYSTERIES

I

My baffled soul, you're still scanning that list of names
for the right angel to talk to,
still searching the kindly shelter of the blossoming
apple tree which once spread wings
in the lower orchard, still
seeking that blue silk dress of childhood swinging
its hem above party shoes.
You can't take no for an answer, you won't
recognize yes.

My silly hands that make mistakes, my eyes
that alight in the wrong places and spend time there
thinking *that's what I want!*—
what next, my tough spreading feet, my knees
the color of mottled moons?

And arrogant heart, all gnarled and sighing,
don't you know none of them exist? Father
is not there, the lover is not here, Grandmother
is leaving. And what of the children?
Those words *you thought less of the little girl*
were told you in a dream. . . .

None of them exist.
I want to pin up my hair in a final farewell
and turn to the sea, or the church tower, for reassurance.
I promise I will call my friend in another town
and ask for his help. I will attempt to visit
the old lady.
And then will you forgive me? You who don't exist?

II

If I kiss you, my life will stop.
So the world comes to take my mouth away.
I must tell you I had a sign
the way, at four years of age, I had chicken pox
in a darkened room. Its refuge
to curl against my grandmother—rocking, rocking.

I wear its mark on my face. I wear this sign
like my thickened ankle I broke when I was drunk.

If I kiss you hard the world as I know it
will stop. Just think—
I may not like it. You may not like.

So the world would stop, and then go on.

III

This morning I watch the sea
the way anyone watches the sea from shore.
I try to open myself
away from fear, let the world
remove my voice.

Aware of a flight of sparrows above tall grass,
I find I like my prepositions
they place me where I am—here—alive
beside the cries of children
at water's edge, beneath
the *asking-asking* noise of gulls,
not far from where a bee
scolds clover for moving in the wind.

This moment, I blame no one for anything
because your face, looking down at me
from a dream, bore the vast
expression of the sky and told me
blame was useless. This moment
the sea enjoys itself and the sky
is simply everywhere above the world.

IV

The man, who was a father, curls against the bedclothes.
He strokes the strap of a watch
for protection, a watch borrowed from the wife
of a dead man. His wide eyes shrug back
from the doorway where his son stands uncertain of words,
of who he sees. The window beyond

stares out at hydrangeas and distressed
summer roses blowing apart in a grey wind.
Inside and outside it's grey. The air above the garden
whirls around, slams at the panes. But the air
above the bed, beside the wardrobe, has stopped short
like an old dog waiting for directions.

The son insists on tea for the man,
rouses him into clothes. The son
tries to shake the air to clarity. The watch,
which is digital and not ticking, looks
for language to persuade: *Get up, go on*
turn toward your flowers which need you.

V
Storybook

The town has fallen through a hole in the lake.
On the bank stand a man and his donkey
staring down through the torn water.
The roofs, steeples, pavements and trees
all keep gliding away. The man
and the donkey blame each other
because all their food, all their friends
have fallen through. But the lake

is lit golden in the late afternoon,
deceptive gold around a beautiful watery throat.
The pines on the ridge go almost black.
it's a long journey into them to the dark
center where fires blaze at the same moment
a seam closes in the lake. The man and the donkey
are left, bewildered, gazing
at the torn pages of their love.

VI

There's a time before anything is sure—
is birdsong bright
or dark, have stones on the beach
been lifted for a reason?

These are pieces of a world I don't inhabit
so I watch the sea, heavy
with moon, rushing at me to say
how dare I contain it with words!

It snorts like many horses all at once,
cares less that I walk
on that silver stain of sand where clouds
reflect their salmon-pink
this certain morning before storms come.

*

There are walls, small spaces, and walls
which we call something else. Television wall,
books, a lover across town.
That change of name between one moment of the self
and another. Most talking is a wall,
certainly the daily phrase. The personal
is a small space, or no space at all
until something calls from the world outside.

*

I hear the sound of rain before it falls, see
the light-coming-down which becomes
that sound. How inexact I am
among the people within these walls.
Rain comes from a world outside.
This moment I live in the wall
of my skull where it's raining.

I want only the dark sound of it—
that thin pure voice to inhabit me.

VII

I want to go out, so it can take me in.
Not fire, earth, water—but air—
my answerable twin.

Let it come into this house which is ready
to blow apart! The wind outside
rattles like that first knowledge
of another person. Inside,
language is just a mouse in the skirting boards.
Let it rush in like a judge
or possible friend. Don't let me fall
through the burning windows.

I'm just a moment in this room
adrift among syllables. My prayers
fall like desire, or flags of rain over the sea.
Notice, the door's unlocked
as for Elijah. I'm ready to lift my face.

from *The Red Window*, 1997

NEW SNOW ON NEW YEAR'S DAY

A rush of radio talk, footsteps:
any daughter needs to walks away
into the bright forest where snow closes,
like an ideal mother
over each branch, twig, and stone—
just soft and thick enough to hold,
or gently fall,
as the child brushes by. Watching
curled mountain laurel leaves
drop their breathy mouthfuls to dimple
a darker path, she lifts
one foot, then another—out
across this momentary, unmarked world.

AGAINST SILENCE

Alone in the field, I touch
where the panicked colt kicked my leg
and feel, deep within my thigh,
the bruise rising. Soon
it will be a harvest of blood
rimming beneath my skin and I'll say *See?*
It hurts! Right here. . . .

*

Decades ago a man in jail, in Watts I think,
needed to show just where the cops
had beat him. How bad it hurt. Locked away
and bruised all over, no one believed him
since he didn't bleed.
What he said was taped and later
a composer looped those words toward a relentless music:
I opened up the bruise
and let the bruise- blood come out
to show them.
          (and I—so crazy for the man
who played that piece for me one gray
Baltimore afternoon—was married.
I'd lied to be with him.)

*

Once or twice a year something hurts
like that and I hear again *come out come*
out to show them—words
layering over themselves
until that song takes shape the way a secret
grows. What's changed
since that daft romantic afternoon?
Despite the bright-eyed pumpkins burning, wind-
thrown leaves, or our assaulted language pleading—

we still bruise and flare.

I rub my leg. Words—those words—or any.
Nothing works until the bruise
opens—

MARTIN

It was just this summer I began to forgive. I was six, all cowlick, mouth, and bones. Those nights he'd slam back home, his fists would crash like stones so I'd wonder which room my head was in. All the coffee, stew, and yelling couldn't help. Our dog, long gone down the cellar stairs, would hide with me if I made it to that one space we shared behind the boiler. We'd curl away till Dad went down hard as an ox and the small house shook toward sleep. When my Mom with her torn hair wept, and his hands left marks along my shoulders and jaw, we all kept silent. Those next raw mornings, what could I do but dream myself a hero? So once I stayed up late with the star-spangled radio and a pile of comics. The flung door cracked the wall behind it as he roared and smashed through the hall, bang-swaying up the stairs past where Mom had locked herself away. He staggered door to door until I heard that bottle roll across the spare room's floor. The bedsprings wailed. When I heard his rasp and snores, I tore off a handful of pages then snuck close and slipped the matches from his coat pocket. I crawled into that small darkness beneath the bed, felt the mattress brush against my hair. As those cartoon faces crumbled, I struck a match and set my father's bed on fire. The air began to craze, my throat tore apart. He tossed and snored while my sudden mother rushed to fix everything before she screamed. I guess I'm sorry, but I remember how warm the space was beneath that bed, a place where my whole body fit and felt briefly safe. That night I began a journey of years away from him. I was six. Look how long it's taken to see my own face repeat and crumble into the glass. Just like his. . . .

1960

The last time I saw him with his fawn crew cut and scuffed
white bucks, Don Armstrong stopped me by my locker and
  said
I need to speak to you later. I have something to tell you.
Those wide gray eyes stopped the breath at my throat.

I forget now why Don was kicked out of school.
Just fourteen, and scared of everything, I fled to books
or curled myself against the pulsing, cinema-dark.
What was he going to say?

His empty seat and those few
curious words, kept him close—one boy
with such white teeth he only danced with cashmere blondes.

Sometimes I think I glimpse him on the street.
He's the face inside the whisky glass, a parable's voice,
and I can't stop hoping that for me
he'd still give up his secret—reveal the world

and one perfect reason for stepping out of it.

FROM THE SUMMER PORCH

I see finches dip along the feeders
or at basin's edge. They know

the sounds a house makes
or when thunder crawls the hills.

Bees, in golden thunder, sift through black-eyed Susans.
As a hawk's shadow stains the clearing

jays, sparrows, cowbirds, doves
spiral up through leaves.

One finch stops to forage in red monarda.
These birds know their world exactly,

where it's best to live and hide.
Each morning I scatter seeds and crumbs

because that yellow bird in scarlet flowers
amazes me. All I am to him

is scent, noise, food. So I hold
these limitations in my arms

for one essential daily moment.

THE RED WINDOW

There, on a gaunt house by the Deerfield River, I saw it—
facing west with its shades drawn.
Perhaps a child is sleeping, savage and ill.

> *It holds to the side*
> *of the house—*
> *it's the hole in the body*
> *where no blood shows.*

*

Both the world and the window are red,
like Christmas.
Or the seepage from tin mines
into ancient seas. Red
as the abraded skin
of infants, and what the cat
leaves beside the barn.

*

Where was that woman standing
when the blind flew up
and the reflected blue leaves of summer
pressed back into the house?
She was looking away toward the river
where once a beaver swam right up to her,
stared hard and slapped
his plank of a tail three times
like some lover, waiting to be restored.

> *In the places where I held him*
> *I discharged my soul. My electric skin*
> *left a shimmer in the churchyard,*
> *attic, on his mother's unmade bed.*

*

It's hard to notice the actual window
when you move about
inside its room. It's an eye where light gushes in. Or stops,
suddenly weighted.

Frenzied birds feed at dawn's chilly edge.

*

The window rinses smooth in the downpour.
A mystery on gray afternoons, it hovers
inside the body's curious shiftings.

Look at those solitary doors closed
on unheated rooms where the very old
stay curled in their beds all winter. Look
at those children playing at the curb—
how their arms, legs, jaws get blown away.

A hole in the sky falls across our cities.

One hole in space is a nest of black eggs, closing forward.
One hole for each of us.

*

Where Penwith's bright peninsula lies down
like a woman, deep in water and wind,
a Cornish painter lived—

after many years of drifting above the *huer's* violet cries,
of seeing rooks, skylarks, gulls, the fields, hedges,
roofs, and crested cliffs clearly from the air—he held still
for one long moment. The land thrust itself against the sky,
pulled the painter in his glider down with jaws of air.
His bones chewed into dirt and stone
while the spirit's eye flickered at window's edge.
            (Peter Lanyon, 1918-1964)

*

I walk into the face of The Gate to the Past,
to that sweet floor strewn with toys.
Children skate by the curb. *Bang-bang,*
like loving all the way through—

*

       they struck me into the wall,
       struck me and left me there and hit my head
       and arms because I was pregnant
       and the watching man comes out of his office.

       He lifts my hair, hitting my head
       on the wall again.
             (*Maria Nikilaidov*)

*

A man and a woman lie side by side.
She wears a loose white cotton slip. Her knees shine
beneath the cell's moon-eyed bulb. He too wears white.
Undershorts and vest. She wonders, how does he wipe
his body? Where are the tissues piling
that keep his nose, feet, and scrotum clean?
What rags touch the tilted corners of his eyes?

There's a hectic in the blood. A soft-bird hex.

She visits and leaves, visits to find the only guard
who was ever nice to them blew his brains out
by the coffee machine. Rust and yellow at the feet
of one inmate in his Thorazine haze.

Who does this window serve? What doors?
       (*M.K., Baker, and Raymond*)

*

Not a world away
a shower of sparrows.
No moon yet.
A boy's arm
in the hedgerow. Air
flooded with noise.
When the soldiers leave,
women wash away their tears
with blood.

*

Back home, a lamp shines behind the shade.
Thin light falls upon the dandelion-grass.
An instant of rose and gold
before dusk eats daytime down to dark.
Hands move about the garden.
Birds hold, hidden and still.

> *Poor mouth, open.*
> *Let a word uncurl your tongue,*
> *or like an insect*
> *brush by mistake*
> *along your inner eye.*

That blue hour, slack gray doves are the last to feed.
A closing. Then the owl from across the river.
What's out there in the caught breath of the forest?

*

The painter soars. We can't
keep him from falling. The skull

is an eye, burnt blind.

On our thick beige-blue bodies, the women
of my family are flecked
with blood-bright dots: torsos, breasts,
arms, and thighs—as though shards
from the red window splintered
through our membranes of skin.

A splatter, weeping from inside out.

*

Sickness fills the wind. The moon's eye shuts.
The window, in stunned repose,
tells the murderer *No!*

And what devil leaps from a dry
to a wet place? Whose serpent
lives curled in the moon's
galactic nest of blood. . . .
The old stories shake out like bedding
scented new as a child's first dreaming.

*

How soft the sea's purple sheen where mackerel
and pilchards feed. The painter flew
and all of us are him falling

by where the salt-blood roses taste sweet
when we meet everything-at-once—
eyes open to an emergency of vision.

*

An inshore wind crawls all the way upriver
where the woman at the window
is the window opening above sweetening air.

                    Sometimes
closing forward, we love—or fly
like the first words of the day spinning
from our teeth. I saw
that window like a person able to speak:
sometimes, able to love.

from *Ghost Farm*, 2010

DAILY

       I have a farm
in Hawley, Massachusetts.
Everything built and done is *daily:*
feeding goats, sheep, chickens, dogs—
the buckets and shovels
       and always that thin architecture
of envelopes, papers, checkbooks, pens.

The farm perches solid and cheerful
on the north side of Hog Mountain (though we are this
year pigless as paradise.)
In cold seasons
its barns and sheds can be seen from the Mohawk Trail.

As I work I feel the distinctly
different nipple of my radiated breast beneath my shirt.
Though the scars begin to fade, the skin
stays blushed and tender.

For eight dragging chemo months
I did few chores. There still are smells
which sicken me: diesel, tea tree oil,
dog and human shit. And scented dryer sheets!

I'm ecstatic now to have an inch of hair!
Most days were quite okay.
Nausea just another kind of job.

       Today I'm joyous in the barn,
mucking out or sorting fleeces. Daily
I salute the funny numbness in my arm:
its freedom of the now I'm in—
glad for chocolate, dogs, for daily breath
and the extending hills beyond.

SOMETIMES

When my mind strays into the world, I do not know who is there. Sometimes,
when my mind comes up against this world, I do not know who is safe.
Sometimes, if I am a passenger in a car driving down Rt. 116,
I can't tell what time I'm in—a child being driven by mother or
    grandparents
towards the house in the country? The young bride with her open heart
    ringed by fear?

If *I* am behind the wheel, I'm the grown-up off to the dentist or taking the dog/
cat/goat to the vet. I might be buying apples or on some errand
of protection and plans.

I couldn't tell that early January evening, blue winter moonlight on snow as we
were passing the cold fields of South Ashfield—I could not tell for a moment
which husband was driving me through the dark. Lurched between times, I
gripped the seat, frantic and without focus until we took the curves and I saw it
was *now,* Mrs. Fuller's barn empty of ponies.

From Brookline to Conway—two hours that were always and forever. Too
long, and since the place *lived* in me, how could it be so far? There was relief
when we'd reach the pastel bales at the Erving paper mill. There I'd bounce
against the seat, sick of it all, both eager and bored.

I'd talk to myself. Finally, on Rt. 116 the tree shadows blacked and un- blacked
the car windows. Eyes closed, I'd see each layer of darkness on my lids as a
shadow-rock. So I'd command the car, like a pony, to jump those shadows and
land on blotches of brightness. The repeated
patterns of sun and dark intrigued me—rhythmic, but not steady.
Once I must have dozed like the grown-ups wanted, sat up and saw a family of
little people waving from the small river's bank. Mom, Dad, and two tiny
children. All the family I wanted. There was even a donkey grazing on ferns. *I
swear this is true!* Today, driving back from Doc's, I could see that curved edge
they waved from. Now a white, tidy house commands their yard and the little
people don't show themselves.

Rt. 116 is a road which stays. It has parts and I can move through them a little
like *the Ghost*. Hands deep in trench coat pockets, head bowed,

he crossed from one side of the bridge to the other. It was that curve in Conway, near the pickle factory—now Orchard Equipment—where Henry worked.

The Ghost was invisible yet solid and I saw him one winter night when I was married and always a passenger.

I may drive, or be driven. The World? Sometimes my mind takes it in.

PAGE BY PAGE

In the child's tipped paperweight, snow drifts behind
the glowing village church into the thick green forest.
Between the pews, a woman in her red
housekeeping smock sweeps away pine needles, dust, hair-
pins and a few scraps of paper. She's humming *O Holy Night.*

At the edge of this picture book, a wolf paces his thicket.
He'd like to curl safely into warm sleep
but hungers instead.

The geese need more than snow to drink so twice a day
the child presses the heavy door outward,
hauls buckets of warm water to the noisy flock.
The paperweight tilts on her dresser.
Most days this child forks the worst of the stained bedding
from the bred ewe's fold, tipping her basket
onto the frozen pile out back. One day, caught in the straw:
a curved spine, wrinkled nut of a head, four hooves
all slathered red. Poor ewe bleating and turning.

Everyone's cold or stuck in small enclosures:
a farm, its fold, the paperweight and page. So the wolf
steps into the white meadow beyond manure steam.
He smells the lamb's blood. You smell it too as your hand
reaches for that cold jug of vodka hidden behind the family Bible.

MUTE

Wearing a dappled blue housekeeping smock
I kneel to wash the floor in that bright
corner room where the secret baby sleeps.

Her wide eyes follow me; her mouth opens
but her cry is collapsed and hidden. I am quiet
with the warm soapy water thin and silent on the tiles.

I'm not supposed to know about this secret child,
even now when I am close to death's long fingers.
Yes, death's thumb presses at my bottom lip.

But this is not about me standing with a bowl of grey water,
wiping my hands on the smock. This is not about
that child curled within a soft yellow blanket.

This is about what passes between us
as I slip out the door dragging death behind me
like a donkey's tail.

A TIBETAN MAN IN HAWLEY, MASSACHUSETTS

Just one step off the edge into the deep
wrong place and a shoe pulls off, is lost.
Amidst twigs, leaves, mosses and stones, this shoe
cannot be found by eyes or strong hands.
Even digging into the exact place the shoe exited its foot,
farther down than the shoe could have delved,
there's no black shoe! What now?
The man stands in thick dry grasses at road's edge
and decides on the one thing children in his village
were taught to do. Slipping off
his other shoe he flings it over to where the first black shoe
must have gone. How long should he wait
for one shoe to find the other? It's August,
too hot to stand for long without flies catching in his hair.
The shoes have tongues; they should call to one another.
It's hot, but the man from Tibet will pace this roadside ditch
waiting for his shoes to rise out of the shadows.

BRINGING BACK THE FARM

So hot the ewe stopped pushing, gave in. The stuck lamb choked off before she got him out. Glistening red knobs on placenta and sac. Still, she had to nuzzle and baa, bring her body back in balance. In these moments I become something else inside. Poor lamb buried, the scooped afterbirth flung safe from dogs into the chicken yard. Delicate frenzied bantams doing a job. Not a scrap left.

If we hadn't pushed the land around, the farm would fall off the north side of Hog Mountain. We had to log, bulldoze, level for building, drill through ledge, undo the forest which ate fields (cleared once in 1802.) Violent pulling apart, smashing of habitat to plant for pasture. Nature out, domestic in.

I yearn to speak charmingly of barn swallows, summer toads (in real barns,) the exasperating whine of fly season, a cria's first pronging in springtime, the smashed flicker, still warm and bleeding brightly from the mouth as we frantically thumb the Field Guide to identify, to save. It's all here, the struggle towards compassion, the pressure to get things done. This farm so vast. For each smile, a sorrow. Still, it's a fortress, a balm. And words don't do the work.

This morning the mouse behind the microwave made it out. The cat going nuts on the countertop spooked that mouse right into my hand. I grabbed its tail. As it curled to bite my finger, I dropped that mouse on the sleeping dog's back, scooped it up again and tossed it out the door. It bounced, then scuttled off.

When I was a poet I carried a pen I could never find. Now a knife in my pocket, twine, grain, syringes—whatever fits. I am always unlatching the gates, the world. In both worlds I keep losing what's necessary to lose.

A soft damp morning. Hard to see through fog. What are those constant birds raucous and cheery? It feels like one big birdness out there, layered and thriving. Nature. On its own, surviving my kind.

How do we find our place in this? Ed's dream: *we had to move to town into a grey tower block. We had to shoot people to access the flat roof. We got to that roof and brought up all our animals but the fencing was no good and one by one they pushed through and fell to the pavement below. Our favorite ones, with names. . .* he saw it through their eyes. The whirling blackness, over and over.

Nature in—some of it out: coccidia, round worms, the wasp's nest inconvenient. A gun waits in case of a rabid fox. A gun no one wants. Most coyotes stay away thanks to seven dogs. Nature in.

Goats, sheep, llamas, alpacas, cattle, ducks, geese, chickens, yaks, and three great heavy beautiful camels. They're in our charge, so as the old phrase goes we bend, fold, spindle and mutilate. We shear, ear tag, hoof-trim, elastrate, inject, tube, paste, hoist, and herd. This husbandry, its battle against parasites and fear. We feed and water; we carry their babies to safety when we can, make sure they nurse. We repair. This motherness, farming! We can only hold so much. It's what we can't contain, their otherness, that we love.

AND YET, SOME DAYS FEEL DIFFERENT

Penelope warps on and every fourth day,
at dusk's unraveling, she cuts
the white wool, slices her knots with a tiny blade,
and then warps on.

The cutting is a truth. And wasteful.
all those thrums, enough for many mattresses.
Even her handsome son who thinks he's so smart
can't figure her out.

There's a lot of guys downstairs, noisy
and on her nerves. Any way you look at it
one war rolls over into another.
Better to cut the warp and wind a new one.

Sometimes she thinks they've beaten her.
If she could run off, she would.
The river comes at her to point the way
but everyone calls her back.

Shear the lambs. Wash, card, spin. The key
to hell is under the mat,
the small lichen-dyed mat she wove as a bride
where the old dog sleeps.

THE STUPA THAT LOBSANG BUILT

Wind has woken and lifts now
above its secret nest of stones.
Breath travels up the golden air
of a strict, but improvising mind.

So many bright findings
and my beloved black cow in a doorway of light.
See? The mathematics of labor blesses everything,
gives it rest on the sure, flat stones

which are not as still as they look.

THE GHOST FARM

is full of moonlight at noon.
The horses have no use for fences.
The barn keeps itself clean
and heavy horses know their job.
When sheep jump, their fleeces fall away
skirted and ready for carding.
Wind blows dust from summer roadsides
into a lace which wraps the apple trees.
The ghost farm is the idea of a man
I loved one night. Our histories of whiskey and skin
drifting through one another
in the cool, open-windowed air.
The farm has thrived, a piece of earth
saved. A place for dogs and cats
to rest after long wandering.
That love I felt is a ghost in the kitchen
making tea, pouring soup for the freezer,
slipping another book into an envelope
for the man I once knew.
Just Wait And See it's called
You'll Like This One Too, its shadow
putting down roots in a newly plowed field.

from *Just Visiting*, 2014

MORE OFTEN THAN NOT

If the door weren't there without her behind it in her smooth
pine green skirt and merino vest, if that door
and its hinges didn't *ahhh* then click its final ½ inch shut, if your heart
didn't feel like a clutch of hot rags caught deep
within your breathing bones then this would not be your life:
its coat rack and starry winter skies, its *ssh ssh* and hiss of wind-filled pines
circling the clearing. Your dog wants in, your dog
wants out and this is a job which steadies your days as you hope
that woman stays across town on her cold, other side of the river.

She is a woman alone who can do as she likes. All day
she chooses one thing then another with no one watching.
It doesn't matter that you love her; your muse
of rough hands and little to say. At noon she spreads her table
with old newspaper and eats chops from her own lambs:
fat, lemon, and mint smearing her fingers.
She is glad of this, making her own edges, and will think of you
only when necessary. Yes, next spring she'll call you
when the old ram catches in the fence and breaks his neck.
You're a fine, useful man and she will give you tea and bread and soft
    cheese.
You will like remembering the taste of that come evening, alone
with your dog and yesterday's soup on the stove.

ALWAYS, THE OLD HOUSE

My grandmother shows me my first yellow rose, pale—called *Moonlight
    Glow—*
which she tends by the stone wall beyond the old, old house.

I shut tight my eyes to see us both in the afternoon light.

There's a tale of *Bereft* in that house which doesn't yet speak of Grandpa
    naked
in the garden, hosing off the sweat and grit of splitting wood. Look!
There's my mother in a red blouse stamping her foot, in tears by the
kitchen door. She and her father are both yelling.

I tilt my head at the phoebe's call, spy on woodchucks in the field
before *Bereft* catches up with me and slips its dry arm around my shoulders.

Late summer is cricket song and the cistern of spring water with its
    graniteware
dipper; it's the scent of apples being cored, chopped then stewed for
    applesauce
which my grandmother sprinkles with red-hots.

Caught in the old walls, the thoughts of this only child crack open the door
while *Bereft* jumps up on the kitchen counter kicking restlessly until,
scolded, she slips down, walks stiffly away across the bright wood floor.

ALMOST SINGING

Under her breath, she rummages for Christmas.
She pauses to watch the snow and thinks of sin and its wolf prints
on the slope back down to the barn. But that was then—
yes, there's always *then* and *now* and the snowscapes of in-between.
Her breath catches. Never bury a child far from the house. Smoothing
that red wool stocking stretched at the toe, she holds it to her cheek.
Never bury a child where she can't hear you singing.

EVEN THE COLD AIR

That smell of salt and smoke
at the back of my mouth
is taste's memory.

I have never lived by a river,
known the life of moving water
as daily climate.

There's a loneliness in this.
I can touch it like a cloak
fallen to the floor. I can hook it to the wall.

*

Two crusts on a green plate
are removed by a woman's hands
and flung out to the geese.

Even in the busy kitchen, the air cools
as a light snow blows across the highway
where three trucks drive into each other.

*

I would like a household of family. Or would I?
Such a thought is an island in my invisible river
but I cannot feel the touch of its seasons.

Even the cold air is on its own. The trees
bare as a sketch in my picture book
and the snow, just an unfolded napkin.

WHEN ELBOW PATCHES

She often thought if she ran into him she'd pretend not to be her.

This morning when she shook the carton of orange juice before pouring it
    out,
she could feel her belly shake too—left to right.

His emails are curmudgeonly.

Once he had captivated her—fair-haired, brown-eyed boy in his green
    corduroy
jacket back when elbow patches were dashing.

His energy had been all nerves.

They shared almost nothing—a couple of dates in the City during school
    breaks
and one evening in bed hushed
in the apartment where, in the next room, his famous father snored.

Her husband snores.

In the mirror her face is thick, splotched. She still has a nice grin.
She knows he's bald now. He was always designed to be bald, that slight
grouchiness and shoulder stoop. She's certain he's invested well.

How he spends his time doesn't much interest her.
When she sees his name in the inbox, it's as though someone's
handing her a cookie, or a ripe scented pear.

She never wants to see him. She never wants him to set eyes on her again.

THEY ARE BREAKING THE HOUSE

shredding the barn, lining up
tiny red blue green toy soldiers for sale.
The grasses have dried to flame;
the stairs are dust and customers roam
all the rooms picking up, putting down
books and cups, silks and soft
eider pillows. Even the mountain
beyond the wide back porch
is up for sale next to the undressed dolls
and bottles of lemon polish.
I walk the hallways calling *It's me—*
Me who was here first! I was the first child!
Why are you selling up?
The brown clapboards still smell
of creosote. Out front, thick maples
swell to green above the jonquil patch.
I turn, dazed—my hands cupped out
as though to catch everything falling away.

JUST VISITING

It's not hard to see
the shadow of life always flickering
even in the dark
flitting to settle in one place
just for a moment.
It dapples along rivers,
on high rises, lawns or
into forests, slithering
its lightness and breath
to stain our multitudes of skin,
bent backs, knees,
office chairs, and open mouths.
The shadow lilts across infants
and the very old who doze
in worn chairs, on pallets, in fluffed
and tidy beds, or curled
beneath an overpass.
When I wake from sleep
this shadow twists along my eyelids,
hardens my feet, warms my hands.
Blessing is all sides of the shadow.

Coda

OCTOBER

My mouth starts speaking in another direction
of how apples are falling into red smoke
and the sun no longer publishes each leaf, or name.

I want to know what's forbidden,
to enter that space
an apple takes from the heart of tree.

From the hills, leaves shiver back
a sound no one can name, speechless
as what's caught behind my teeth.

Dark radiance, your hands have unpeeled this story
to the edge of the world!
It falls against a man turning

to look back on a year, on a field
where blue deer descend
stitching the heartland up for winter.

The branches now fill up with sky
holding that horizon empty of me
where a man

Slowly opens his hands
as deer lie down where leaf and fruit
must sleep forever.

About Jody Stewart

JODY STEWART (aka Pamela Stewart) began writing because she couldn't draw. Over the years, she's published 5 chapbooks, 6 longer poetry collections, taught at ASU, Univ, of Arizona, UC Irvine and University of Houston. A Guggenheim took her to St. Ives, Cornwall where she lived for 7 half-magical years before landing back in western Massachusetts where she lives on a retired farm with a few animals including a rescue race horse, his donkey, and an emu named Nigel.

Made in the USA
Middletown, DE
20 November 2022

15108589R00097